AUTO
MILEAGE TRACKER

Copyright 2014

All Rights reserved. No part of this book may be reproduced or used in any way or form or by any means whether electronic or mechanical, this means that you cannot record or photocopy any material ideas or tips that are provided in this book.

MILEAGE TRACKER

DATE	ODOMETER	GALLONS	MILES	MPG	COMMENT

MILEAGE TRACKER

DATE	ODOMETER	GALLONS	MILES	MPG	COMMENT

MILEAGE TRACKER

DATE	ODOMETER	GALLONS	MILES	MPG	COMMENT

MILEAGE TRACKER

DATE	ODOMETER	GALLONS	MILES	MPG	COMMENT

MILEAGE TRACKER

DATE	ODOMETER	GALLONS	MILES	MPG	COMMENT

MILEAGE TRACKER

DATE	ODOMETER	GALLONS	MILES	MPG	COMMENT

MILEAGE TRACKER

DATE	ODOMETER	GALLONS	MILES	MPG	COMMENT

MILEAGE TRACKER

DATE	ODOMETER	GALLONS	MILES	MPG	COMMENT
DATE	ODOMETER	GALLONS	MILES	MPG	COMMENT

MILEAGE TRACKER

DATE	ODOMETER	GALLONS	MILES	MPG	COMMENT

MILEAGE TRACKER

DATE	ODOMETER	GALLONS	MILES	MPG	COMMENT
DATE	ODOMETER	GALLONS	MILES	MPG	COMMENT

MILEAGE TRACKER

DATE	ODOMETER	GALLONS	MILES	MPG	COMMENT

MILEAGE TRACKER

DATE	ODOMETER	GALLONS	MILES	MPG	COMMENT

MILEAGE TRACKER

DATE	ODOMETER	GALLONS	MILES	MPG	COMMENT

MILEAGE TRACKER

DATE	ODOMETER	GALLONS	MILES	MPG	COMMENT

MILEAGE TRACKER

DATE	ODOMETER	GALLONS	MILES	MPG	COMMENT

MILEAGE TRACKER

DATE	ODOMETER	GALLONS	MILES	MPG	COMMENT

MILEAGE TRACKER

DATE	ODOMETER	GALLONS	MILES	MPG	COMMENT

MILEAGE TRACKER

DATE	ODOMETER	GALLONS	MILES	MPG	COMMENT

MILEAGE TRACKER

DATE	ODOMETER	GALLONS	MILES	MPG	COMMENT

MILEAGE TRACKER

DATE	ODOMETER	GALLONS	MILES	MPG	COMMENT

MILEAGE TRACKER

DATE	ODOMETER	GALLONS	MILES	MPG	COMMENT

MILEAGE TRACKER

DATE	ODOMETER	GALLONS	MILES	MPG	COMMENT

MILEAGE TRACKER

DATE	ODOMETER	GALLONS	MILES	MPG	COMMENT

MILEAGE TRACKER

DATE	ODOMETER	GALLONS	MILES	MPG	COMMENT

MILEAGE TRACKER

DATE	ODOMETER	GALLONS	MILES	MPG	COMMENT

MILEAGE TRACKER

DATE	ODOMETER	GALLONS	MILES	MPG	COMMENT

MILEAGE TRACKER

DATE	ODOMETER	GALLONS	MILES	MPG	COMMENT

MILEAGE TRACKER

DATE	ODOMETER	GALLONS	MILES	MPG	COMMENT

MILEAGE TRACKER

DATE	ODOMETER	GALLONS	MILES	MPG	COMMENT

MILEAGE TRACKER

DATE	ODOMETER	GALLONS	MILES	MPG	COMMENT

MILEAGE TRACKER

DATE	ODOMETER	GALLONS	MILES	MPG	COMMENT

MILEAGE TRACKER

DATE	ODOMETER	GALLONS	MILES	MPG	COMMENT

MILEAGE TRACKER

DATE	ODOMETER	GALLONS	MILES	MPG	COMMENT

MILEAGE TRACKER

DATE	ODOMETER	GALLONS	MILES	MPG	COMMENT

MILEAGE TRACKER

DATE	ODOMETER	GALLONS	MILES	MPG	COMMENT

MILEAGE TRACKER

DATE	ODOMETER	GALLONS	MILES	MPG	COMMENT

MILEAGE TRACKER

DATE	ODOMETER	GALLONS	MILES	MPG	COMMENT

MILEAGE TRACKER

DATE	ODOMETER	GALLONS	MILES	MPG	COMMENT

MILEAGE TRACKER

DATE	ODOMETER	GALLONS	MILES	MPG	COMMENT

MILEAGE TRACKER

DATE	ODOMETER	GALLONS	MILES	MPG	COMMENT

MILEAGE TRACKER

DATE	ODOMETER	GALLONS	MILES	MPG	COMMENT

MILEAGE TRACKER

DATE	ODOMETER	GALLONS	MILES	MPG	COMMENT

MILEAGE TRACKER

DATE	ODOMETER	GALLONS	MILES	MPG	COMMENT

MILEAGE TRACKER

DATE	ODOMETER	GALLONS	MILES	MPG	COMMENT

MILEAGE TRACKER

DATE	ODOMETER	GALLONS	MILES	MPG	COMMENT

MILEAGE TRACKER

DATE	ODOMETER	GALLONS	MILES	MPG	COMMENT

MILEAGE TRACKER

DATE	ODOMETER	GALLONS	MILES	MPG	COMMENT

MILEAGE TRACKER

DATE	ODOMETER	GALLONS	MILES	MPG	COMMENT

MILEAGE TRACKER

DATE	ODOMETER	GALLONS	MILES	MPG	COMMENT

MILEAGE TRACKER

DATE	ODOMETER	GALLONS	MILES	MPG	COMMENT

MILEAGE TRACKER

DATE	ODOMETER	GALLONS	MILES	MPG	COMMENT

MILEAGE TRACKER

DATE	ODOMETER	GALLONS	MILES	MPG	COMMENT

MILEAGE TRACKER

DATE	ODOMETER	GALLONS	MILES	MPG	COMMENT

MILEAGE TRACKER

DATE	ODOMETER	GALLONS	MILES	MPG	COMMENT

MILEAGE TRACKER

DATE	ODOMETER	GALLONS	MILES	MPG	COMMENT

MILEAGE TRACKER

DATE	ODOMETER	GALLONS	MILES	MPG	COMMENT

MILEAGE TRACKER

DATE	ODOMETER	GALLONS	MILES	MPG	COMMENT

MILEAGE TRACKER

DATE	ODOMETER	GALLONS	MILES	MPG	COMMENT

MILEAGE TRACKER

DATE	ODOMETER	GALLONS	MILES	MPG	COMMENT

MILEAGE TRACKER

DATE	ODOMETER	GALLONS	MILES	MPG	COMMENT

MILEAGE TRACKER

DATE	ODOMETER	GALLONS	MILES	MPG	COMMENT

MILEAGE TRACKER

DATE	ODOMETER	GALLONS	MILES	MPG	COMMENT

MILEAGE TRACKER

DATE	ODOMETER	GALLONS	MILES	MPG	COMMENT

MILEAGE TRACKER

DATE	ODOMETER	GALLONS	MILES	MPG	COMMENT

MILEAGE TRACKER

DATE	ODOMETER	GALLONS	MILES	MPG	COMMENT

MILEAGE TRACKER

DATE	ODOMETER	GALLONS	MILES	MPG	COMMENT

MILEAGE TRACKER

DATE	ODOMETER	GALLONS	MILES	MPG	COMMENT

MILEAGE TRACKER

DATE	ODOMETER	GALLONS	MILES	MPG	COMMENT

MILEAGE TRACKER

DATE	ODOMETER	GALLONS	MILES	MPG	COMMENT

MILEAGE TRACKER

DATE	ODOMETER	GALLONS	MILES	MPG	COMMENT

MILEAGE TRACKER

DATE	ODOMETER	GALLONS	MILES	MPG	COMMENT

MILEAGE TRACKER

DATE	ODOMETER	GALLONS	MILES	MPG	COMMENT

MILEAGE TRACKER

DATE	ODOMETER	GALLONS	MILES	MPG	COMMENT

MILEAGE TRACKER

DATE	ODOMETER	GALLONS	MILES	MPG	COMMENT

MILEAGE TRACKER

DATE	ODOMETER	GALLONS	MILES	MPG	COMMENT

MILEAGE TRACKER

DATE	ODOMETER	GALLONS	MILES	MPG	COMMENT

MILEAGE TRACKER

DATE	ODOMETER	GALLONS	MILES	MPG	COMMENT

MILEAGE TRACKER

DATE	ODOMETER	GALLONS	MILES	MPG	COMMENT

MILEAGE TRACKER

DATE	ODOMETER	GALLONS	MILES	MPG	COMMENT

MILEAGE TRACKER

DATE	ODOMETER	GALLONS	MILES	MPG	COMMENT

MILEAGE TRACKER

DATE	ODOMETER	GALLONS	MILES	MPG	COMMENT

MILEAGE TRACKER

DATE	ODOMETER	GALLONS	MILES	MPG	COMMENT

MILEAGE TRACKER

DATE	ODOMETER	GALLONS	MILES	MPG	COMMENT

MILEAGE TRACKER

DATE	ODOMETER	GALLONS	MILES	MPG	COMMENT

MILEAGE TRACKER

DATE	ODOMETER	GALLONS	MILES	MPG	COMMENT

MILEAGE TRACKER

DATE	ODOMETER	GALLONS	MILES	MPG	COMMENT

MILEAGE TRACKER

DATE	ODOMETER	GALLONS	MILES	MPG	COMMENT

MILEAGE TRACKER

DATE	ODOMETER	GALLONS	MILES	MPG	COMMENT

MILEAGE TRACKER

DATE	ODOMETER	GALLONS	MILES	MPG	COMMENT

MILEAGE TRACKER

DATE	ODOMETER	GALLONS	MILES	MPG	COMMENT

MILEAGE TRACKER

DATE	ODOMETER	GALLONS	MILES	MPG	COMMENT

MILEAGE TRACKER

DATE	ODOMETER	GALLONS	MILES	MPG	COMMENT
DATE	ODOMETER	GALLONS	MILES	MPG	COMMENT

MILEAGE TRACKER

DATE	ODOMETER	GALLONS	MILES	MPG	COMMENT

MILEAGE TRACKER

DATE	ODOMETER	GALLONS	MILES	MPG	COMMENT

MILEAGE TRACKER

DATE	ODOMETER	GALLONS	MILES	MPG	COMMENT

MILEAGE TRACKER

DATE	ODOMETER	GALLONS	MILES	MPG	COMMENT

MILEAGE TRACKER

DATE	ODOMETER	GALLONS	MILES	MPG	COMMENT

MILEAGE TRACKER

DATE	ODOMETER	GALLONS	MILES	MPG	COMMENT

www.ingramcontent.com/pod-product-compliance
Lightning Source LLC
Chambersburg PA
CBHW081949160726
47999CB00008B/2564